.

PHYSICAL
SCIENCE
PROJECTS
★ for Kids ★

A PROJECT GUIDE TO

ELECTRICITY
AND
MAGNETISM

Colleen Kessler

Mitchell Lane

P.O. Box 196
Hockessin, Delaware 19707
Visit us on the web: www.mitchelllane.com
Comments? email us: mitchelllane@mitchelllane.com

Mitchell Lane

PHYSICAL SCIENCE PROJECTS
☆ for kids ☆

A Project Guide to:
Chemistry • **Electricity and Magnetism**
Forces and Motion • Light and Optics
Matter • Sound

Copyright © 2012 by Mitchell Lane Publishers

All rights reserved. No part of this book may be reproduced without written permission from the publisher. Printed and bound in the United States of America.

Library of Congress
Cataloging-in-Publication Data
Kessler, Colleen.
 A project guide to electricity and magnetism / Colleen D. Kessler.
    p. cm. — (Physical science projects for kids)
 Includes bibliographical references and index.
 ISBN 978-1-58415-966-7 (lib. bd.)
 1. Electricity—Experiments—Juvenile literature. 2. Magnetism—Experiments—Juvenile literature. 3. Science projects—Juvenile literature. I. Title.
 QC527.2.K476 2011
 537—dc22
                                    2011000722

Printing   1   2   3   4   5   6   7   8   9

eBook ISBN: 9781612281087

PLB

CONTENTS

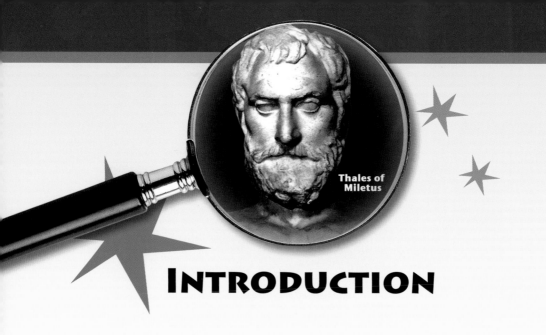
Thales of Miletus

INTRODUCTION

What do you do after a long day at school? Grab a snack and pop it in the microwave? Flip the light switch in the family room, push the button to the video game console, and play your latest game for an hour? While people of many cultures do without electricity on a daily basis, most of us simply take it for granted. We constantly use the many items it powers.

Whom can we thank for this amazing invention that some of us use every day? Was it Benjamin Franklin and his famous kite experiment? Thomas Edison and his electric company? The truth is, nobody *invented* electricity. It has always been around. It has taken the work of many scientists, and hundreds of years, to describe it and fine-tune its use. In fact, we are still learning about electricity.

In 600 BCE, Greek philosopher Thales of Miletus (c. 624–c. 547 BCE) discovered that if he rubbed silk on amber, the amber attracted lightweight objects such as dust and feathers. The Greek word for amber is *elektron*. In 1600 CE—2,200 years later—William Gilbert (1544–1603) studied Thales' experiments. He used the Greek word for amber to make up the term *electricity*. Gilbert realized that electricity and magnetism are related. These early discoveries led to many experiments with static electricity, magnetism, and eventually current electricity.

All matter is made of tiny particles called atoms. These atoms are made up of protons, electrons, and most of the time neutrons. (The hydrogen atom has no neutrons.) Protons, electrons, and neutrons have

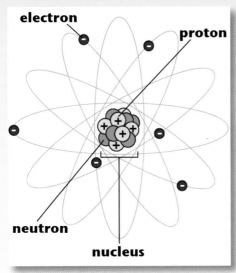

electron

proton

neutron

nucleus

different properties from one another. One of these differences is something called a charge, which is the amount of electrical energy something has. Protons have a positive charge. Electrons have a negative charge. Neutrons do not have a charge.

Atoms usually have the same number of protons and electrons. Those that do are called neutral. When objects are rubbed together, though, electrons can jump from one object to another, giving some atoms more or fewer electrons than protons. Those with more electrons are negatively charged. Those with more protons are positively charged. Objects with opposite charges have "static electricity" and attract one another. This is where the saying "opposites attract" comes from.

Have you ever taken off your winter hat and found that your hair is sticking up? Your hat rubs against your hair when you pull it off. Electrons are transferred from your hair to the hat. Now each of your hairs has the same charge. Since like charges repel each other, each hair is trying to get as far away as it can from all the other hairs. This repulsion causes your hair to stand up.

In 1752, Benjamin Franklin (1706– 1790) proved that lightning is a form of electricity by flying a kite in a storm. The silk kite had a metal wire at the tip, and the string had a metal key tied to it. The metal wire attracted electricity from the lightning, and the loose threads on the string stuck out. When he placed his knuckle close to the key, he detected an electric spark. *Do not try this yourself!* Franklin was lucky that he wasn't killed.

Electricity was a hobby for Franklin, and he wanted to understand it better. His work inspired others to learn more about it too.

In 1780, Italian biologist Luigi Galvani (1737–1798) learned about electricity in the body. While dissecting a frog, he discovered that when he touched the metal scalpel he was using to the frog's leg, its muscles twitched. An electrical charge traveled from one metal object (the scalpel) through the nerve in the frog's leg to another metal object (the steel tray). He called the muscle's reaction "animal electricity."

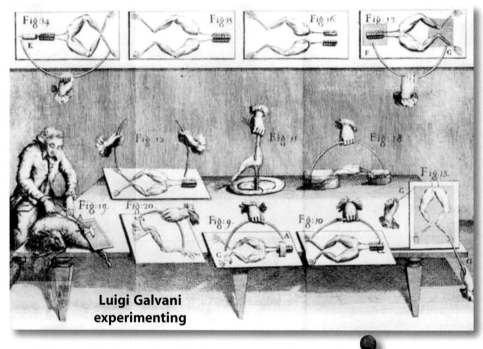

Luigi Galvani experimenting

Using this information, Italian scientist Alessandro Volta (1745–1827) created the first battery in the early 1800s. He used metal disks with wet muslin (a type of cloth) sandwiched between them. Soon after that, in 1820, Hans Christian Oersted (1777–1851) discovered that electrical charges could produce magnetism. French physicist André Ampère (1775–1836) continued Oersted's work. He, too, was interested in understanding the relationship between electricity and magnetism.

Alessandro Volta's battery

Hans Christian Oersted

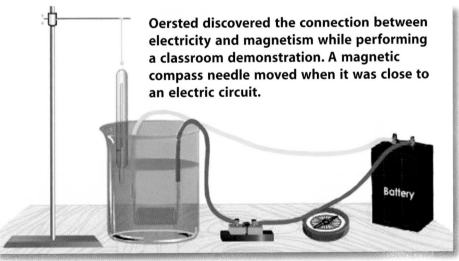

Oersted discovered the connection between electricity and magnetism while performing a classroom demonstration. A magnetic compass needle moved when it was close to an electric circuit.

André Ampère

Illustration of Ampère's apparatus from *Mémoire présenté à l'Académie royale des sciences* (*Memoir Presented to the Royal Academy of Sciences*), published in 1820

The inside of an ammeter, which measures amperes (amps). A. Large magnet. B. Soft-iron keeper magnetized by magnet and acting as resistance. D. Cylinder turning within B, and actuated by current entering at C1, and flowing through spiral wire (not shown) at base of D, and through coil on cylinder to terminal C2. E. Hair-spring regulating pointer. F. Pointer stops.

The 1800s were a time full of discoveries related to the work of these and other scientists. The properties of electricity and magnetism that they discovered led to many exciting inventions. Among them are the telegraph, the refrigerator, the telephone, and the computer.

In this book you'll learn more about the connections these scientists discovered. You'll have a chance to build, create, and experiment with electricity and magnets. Before you start the projects in this book, remember to read the instructions carefully, all the way through. If the directions tell you to have an adult help you, please do so. Be sure to record your procedure and all data, including the date and time of the experiment, in a science notebook. That way you can go back later and look for connections in your own work.

Most of these activities use common materials that you can find around the house. However, if you enjoy working with batteries, bulbs, and wires, you may want some additional materials. Bulbs, bulb holders, battery holders, insulated wire with clip leads, switches, and simple buzzers can be ordered for a dollar or two apiece from home and school science supply companies. A few of these suppliers are listed on page 45.

When we tried out these activities before including them in this book, we did them both ways. We tried them with common materials *and* with holders and switches. Both worked well. You may see photos of both methods as you read.

Whenever you work with electricity or magnets, use common sense. Do not put things in or near your mouth, and follow all instructions. Put only approved electrical connectors in household outlets. All the experiments in this book use household batteries, so they are safe. Have fun!

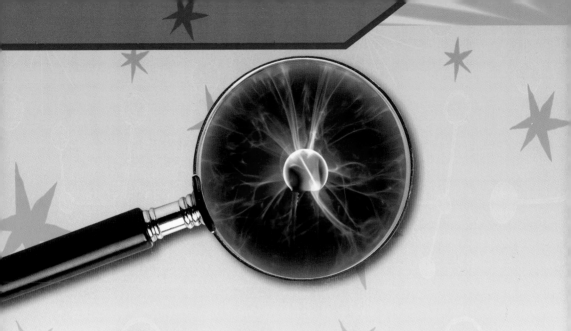

BITS OF LIGHTNING

You may have seen flashes of light or sparks when your pajamas have rubbed against your blankets at night. These sparks are caused by static electricity. When your clothes rub against the blankets, electrons move from one fabric to the other, and charges build up. The sparks happen when the charges are released and the fabrics return to neutral.

During storms, you can see giant sparks of static electricity—lightning. Moving air makes ice and water droplets in clouds rub together. They become charged with static electricity. The positively charged particles rise to the top of the cloud. The negatively charged particles move to the bottom of the cloud. These negatively charged particles are attracted to the positively charged particles in other clouds or on the ground. When the charges build enough, they are released as lightning.

In this activity, you can harness the power of static electricity to make your own lightning.

Instructions
1. Place a metal tray on a table.
2. Turn the lights off in the room, then stand next to the tray or to the doorknob.

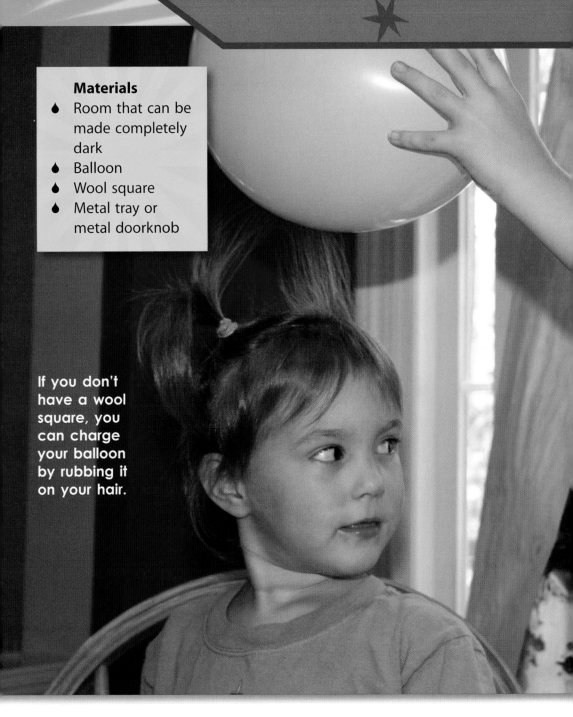

Materials
- Room that can be made completely dark
- Balloon
- Wool square
- Metal tray or metal doorknob

If you don't have a wool square, you can charge your balloon by rubbing it on your hair.

3. Blow up a balloon. Rub it as fast as you can with the wool square.
4. Move your balloon next to the metal tray or doorknob and watch closely. You should see a small spark of lightning—static electricity—jump between the balloon and the metal.

Gold Leaf Electroscope

ALUMINUM-LEAF ELECTROSCOPE

An electroscope is an instrument that can be used to test objects for electrical charges. William Gilbert invented the first electroscope in 1600. Called a versorium, it had a metal needle that could move freely. If a charged object came near, the needle would turn toward it.

Throughout the 1600s and 1700s, the electroscope went through many changes. A hanging thread was added. This thread was attracted to charged objects nearby. Later, tiny balls made out of plant fibers called pith were added to the ends of the thread. The balls would become charged when they were placed near charged objects. Since they would gain the same charge, they would repel each other. How far apart they spread indicated the strength of the charge.

William Gilbert's versorium needle electroscope

Around 1786 or 1787, the electroscope was fine-tuned further. Strips of gold foil, called leaves, were used because gold is much more sensitive than thread or the tiny pith balls. You can use aluminum foil to make an electroscope similar to the gold-leaf electroscope. Use it to check for static electricity around you.

Instructions
1. Ask **an adult** to poke a hole in the lid of a jar. Suggest that the adult use a hammer and nail or a small hand drill.
2. Straighten a paper clip and push it through the hole in the jar lid. Bend the end of the paper clip that will be inside the jar into an L.
3. Use modeling clay on the outside and inside of the lid to hold the paper clip in place.
4. Roll a piece of aluminum foil into a ball the size of a golf ball. Push it onto the

The ends of the aluminum foil strip will move when the foil ball gets close to static electricity.

Charge the balloon,
then put it next to
the electroscope.

straight end of the paper clip. This will be outside the jar when the lid is on.

5. Cut a 4-inch by 1/2-inch strip of aluminum foil and fold it over the L part of the paper clip.

6. Put the lid on the jar and close it tightly to seal the foil strip inside.

7. Blow up a balloon. Rub it as quickly as you can on a wool square.

8. Take it away from the wool and hold it close to the aluminum ball. You should see the ends of the foil strip inside the jar moving apart as the static electricity travels from your balloon through the paper clip and down to the strips.

9. Now experiment with your electroscope. What things do you have in the house that may have an electrical charge? Your TV monitor? DVD player? Hairbrush? Carpet? Write a list of things you think may have a charge in your science notebook, then test your hypotheses. Don't forget to record your results!

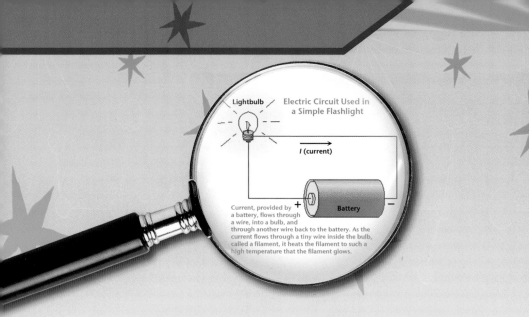

Lightbulb / Electric Circuit Used in a Simple Flashlight

I (current)

+ Battery −

Current, provided by a battery, flows through a wire, into a bulb, and through another wire back to the battery. As the current flows through a tiny wire inside the bulb, called a filament, it heats the filament to such a high temperature that the filament glows.

SIMPLE CIRCUIT

Static electricity is a build-up of charges on a surface. The charges stay on that object until they are transferred to another object—as with the spark in the first experiment. Another type is current electricity. Current electricity is moving electricity.

In order for electricity to work, it must run through a circuit. A circuit is an unbroken path through which an electrical current can flow. Some circuits are very simple (such as in a flashlight), and others very complex (such as in a computer). No matter how complicated they are, all circuits work in the same way.

Electricity leaves one end of the power source. It travels a path. Then it returns to the other end of the power source in an unbroken loop. In your flashlight, the electricity leaves the negative end of the battery and travels through the wires to the bulb, then through more wires and back to the positive end of the battery.

Have you ever noticed that most electrical plugs have two prongs? When the plug is connected to the electrical outlet, electricity flows in through one prong, down one wire to the device that needs power, and then out through the other wire and prong.

Watch as the bulb lights up.

Instructions

1. Cut two strips of aluminum foil. Tape one strip to the positive end of a battery. Tape the other strip to the negative end of the same battery.
2. Touch the free end of the strip attached to the positive end of the battery to the metal just below the glass on the bulb.
3. Touch the free end of the other foil strip to the silver tip on the bottom of the bulb.
4. Your bulb should light up. You have created an unbroken path for the electricity—a complete circuit.
5. What will happen if you add a second battery? How can you connect it?
6. Does the direction in which you connect the second battery matter?

Your bulb should glow brighter with two batteries, because the extra battery adds more power to the circuit. You need to connect the batteries' positive ends to their negative ends for the circuit to work.

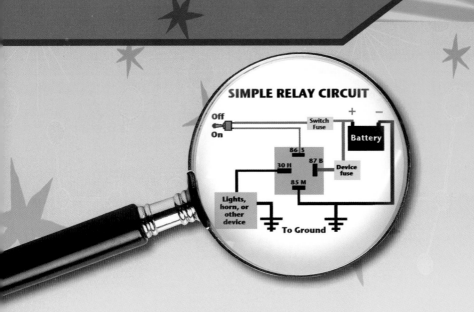

SIMPLE RELAY CIRCUIT

Off / On

Switch Fuse

+ −

Battery

86 S

30 H   87 B

85 M

Device fuse

Lights, horn, or other device

To Ground

SWITCH IT UP

The flow of electricity is called a current. As you learned in the previous activity, items that need electricity get it from a power source, such as a battery (direct current—DC) or an electrical outlet (alternating current—AC). The electricity flows from the power source through a conductor to the object and back to the power source. If the circuit is broken for any reason, the item will not work.

Most electrical items have a switch that completes or breaks a circuit. The circuit is complete when the switch is closed. Then electricity can travel to and from the power source.

In this activity, you'll add a switch to your circuit. You can use a premade switch, or you can make your own using thumbtacks and a paper clip.

Instructions
1. Use one piece of wire to connect the bulb holder to the positive end of the battery.
2. Connect one end of another wire to the negative end of the battery. Connect the other end to a switch, or wrap it around a thumbtack. Push the thumbtack through the end of a paper clip and into a piece of wood.

Materials
- Switch or the following materials:
  - Small piece of lightweight wood such as balsa
  - Two metal thumbtacks
  - Large metal paper clip
- Three pieces insulated wire
- Bulb
- Bulb holder
- D-cell battery
- Battery holder
- Metal paper clip

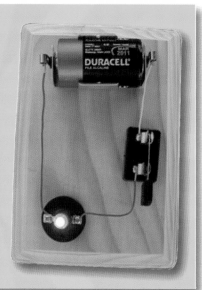

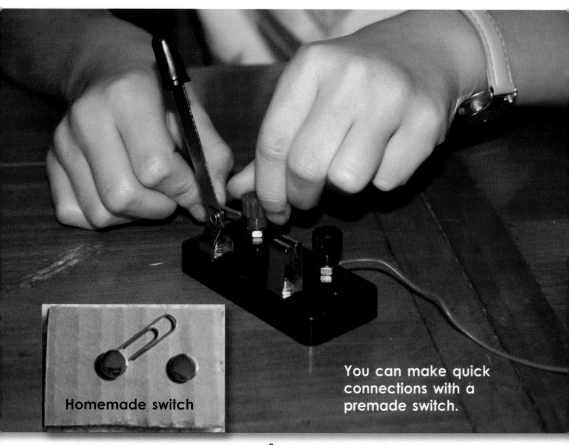

Homemade switch

You can make quick connections with a premade switch.

When the circuit is closed, the bulb will light.

3. Connect one end of the last piece of wire to the other side of the bulb holder. Wrap the other end tightly around a second thumbtack.
4. Push the second thumbtack into the wood across from the first tack, close enough for the paper clip to touch it.
5. Light the bulb by closing the switch—turn the paper clip so that it touches the second tack. This completes the circuit, and electricity can run from the battery to the bulb and back again.

Joseph Swan
lightbulb

Thomas
Edison
lightbulb

QUIZ TIME!

Like any of the great inventions, the lightbulb is the result of the work of many people. Inventors searched for ways to convert electricity into light beginning in the early 1800s. Sir Humphry Davy (1778–1829) passed a current through platinum strips in 1801. The strips glowed, but then vaporized. Each time, the light would last only a few seconds. He invented the arc lamp in 1809. This was made up of two charcoal rods connected to a battery. It was small but glowed brightly.

In 1840, Warren de la Rue (1815–1889) created a bulb made with a platinum coil inside a vacuum tube. This worked well, but platinum is expensive. Most people would not be able to use a bulb like this.

Joseph Wilson Swan (1828–1914) worked hard to create a long-lasting but inexpensive bulb. In 1878, he used a

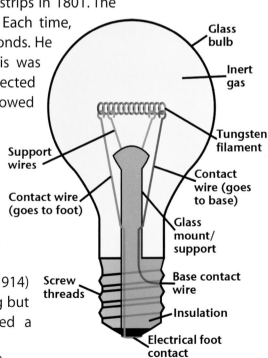

Glass bulb

Inert gas

Tungsten filament

Support wires

Contact wire (goes to base)

Contact wire (goes to foot)

Glass mount/ support

Screw threads

Base contact wire

Insulation

Electrical foot contact

carbon paper filament inside his bulbs. A filament is a thin wire that is superheated by electricity to make light.

Swan was successful. By 1880, he was selling his bulbs to people all over Europe. Thomas Edison is usually the one we remember as inventing it, though. While Swan worked in England, Edison worked in the United States. He wanted to invent a bulb that would shine bright for a long time. Eventually he was able to create a bulb that glowed for 1,200 hours. His incandescent design—a filament in glass with a screw-in base—is still used today.

You can use Edison's invention to create a quiz game.

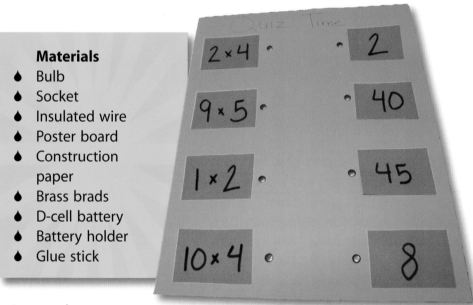

Materials
- Bulb
- Socket
- Insulated wire
- Poster board
- Construction paper
- Brass brads
- D-cell battery
- Battery holder
- Glue stick

Instructions
1. Write some questions and answers, each on a separate square of paper. They could be trivia questions, math questions, or study questions for school.
2. Glue the questions in one column on the poster board.
3. Glue the answers in a random order in another column on the poster board.
4. Push a brad through the board next to each question and answer.
5. Flip the poster board over. Use short pieces of wire to connect the fastener by each question to the fastener by the correct answer.
6. Make a circuit using a battery in a holder, a bulb in a socket, and two additional pieces of wire. Leave the ends of the wire free.

Back of
the project
board

7. Ask a friend a question. With one free wire tip, touch the question.
8. With the other free wire tip, touch the answer your friend gives. If your friend is correct, the wires will complete the circuit and the bulb will light. If your friend is incorrect, the bulb will not light.

The bulb will light only when the question is connected to the right answer.

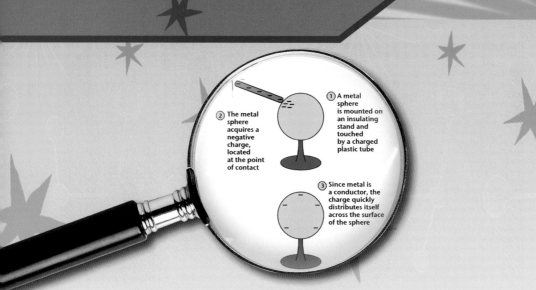

① A metal sphere is mounted on an insulating stand and touched by a charged plastic tube

② The metal sphere acquires a negative charge, located at the point of contact

③ Since metal is a conductor, the charge quickly distributes itself across the surface of the sphere

CONDUCTORS AND INSULATORS

Some substances carry (conduct) electricity better than others. These materials are called conductors. Substances that do not carry electricity, or that carry it poorly, are called insulators. You have been using insulated wire in these experiments. The metal wire is a good conductor. The coating on the wire insulates it, keeping the electricity flowing along its circuit within the wire.

You make a path for electricity to travel when you connect a good conductor to a battery. Insulators, on the other hand, act as a barrier to electricity. It is important to know what materials are good conductors and which are good insulators. In this activity, you will test several different materials to find out how well they conduct electricity.

Materials
- Three pieces insulated wire
- D-cell battery
- Battery holder
- Bulb
- Bulb Holder
- Objects to test, such as glass, plastic, rubber, metal, and wood

Will a plastic pen conduct electricity?

Instructions

1. Connect one end of a piece of wire to the negative end of the battery in the holder. Connect the other end to the bulb holder.
2. Connect another piece of wire to the other side of the battery.
3. Connect the final piece of wire to the open side of the bulb holder.
4. Touch the two open ends of wire to each other to make sure the bulb works. Then touch them to one of the items you wish to test. Does the bulb light up? If it does, the item is a good conductor. If it does not, the item is an insulator.
5. Test each of your other objects in the same way, and record your results.

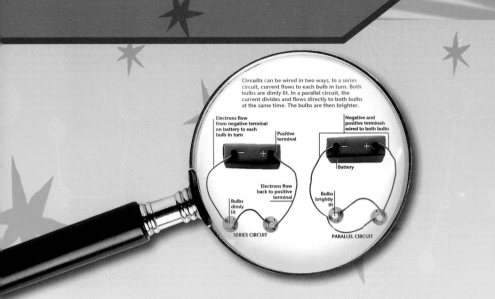

Circuits can be wired in two ways. In a series circuit, current flows to each bulb in turn. Both bulbs are dimly lit. In a parallel circuit, the current divides and flows directly to both bulbs at the same time. The bulbs are then brighter.

Electrons flow from negative terminal on battery to each bulb in turn

Positive terminal

Negative and positive terminals wired to both bulbs

Battery

Electrons flow back to positive terminal

Bulbs dimly lit

Bulbs brightly lit

SERIES CIRCUIT

PARALLEL CIRCUIT

DIFFERENT TYPES OF CIRCUITS

You have built several simple circuits that contain one lightbulb. What would happen if you added another bulb? If two bulbs use the power from a single battery, the lights would be dimmer than if only one bulb were using it. A bulb is like a little bridge that electricity crosses on its way from and back to its power source. The electrons slow down as they cross, then they head back to the battery.

The second bulb slows the electrons even further. They have two bridges to cross now, and twice the work to do. They are not able to light the bulbs brightly. A third bulb will dim the lights even further.

There are different ways you could hook up the two bulbs to your circuit. You could add another wire and keep the bulbs and batteries in a line. This is called a series circuit.

Adding more batteries to your circuit will also add more power. Battery power is measured in volts. A D-cell has 1.5 volts. Two D-cells provide 3.0 volts.

The biggest problem with a series circuit is that if one bulb goes out, all of them will go out. Remember that electrons need a complete circuit to flow. If there is a break in the circuit, the flow will stop. There is another way to wire a circuit so that this does not happen. A parallel circuit gives each bulb its own little circuit; and each one has its own source of power.

Materials
- Three bulbs
- Three bulb holders
- Seven pieces insulated wire
- Two batteries
- Two battery holders
- Switch

Instructions
1. Place three bulbs in bulb holders. Connect the bulbs in a row. This is called a series.
2. Add the batteries and the switch to the series.
3. Close the switch to light the bulbs. How bright are they?
4. Loosen one bulb. What happens? The other bulbs should go out.

How bright are bulbs in a series circuit?

Connect the bulbs in parallel circuits. Are they brighter now?

5. Disconnect the wires.
6. Connect one side of each bulb holder using two wires. Connect the other side of the bulb holders using another two wires.
7. Add another wire between the positive end of one battery to the switch.
8. Connect the negative end of that battery to the positive end of the other battery.
9. Connect another wire from the switch to the side of the first bulb holder.
10. Add another wire between the negative end of the second battery to the first bulb holder.
11. Close the switch. How bright are the bulbs? How does this compare with the series circuit?
12. Loosen one bulb. What happens? Do all the bulbs go out when one is loosened? They shouldn't. Remember that in a parallel circuit, each bulb has its own circuit. When one bulb breaks, the other bulbs still work.

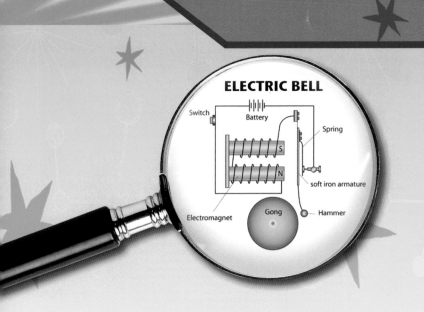

ELECTRIC BELL

Switch

Battery

Spring

S

N

soft iron armature

Electromagnet

Gong

Hammer

ROOM ALARM

Batteries, bulbs, buzzers, and some wire can be used to create many different things. Now you have an understanding of how electricity flows. Experiment by adding batteries to give more power. Add bulbs or buzzers. Make a toy car move with an electric motor. Or, create this alarm so you know when your brother or sister sneaks into your room!

Materials
- D-cell battery
- Battery holder
- Three pieces insulated wire
- Poster board
- Aluminum foil
- Duct tape
- Scissors
- Ruler
- Small buzzer (available at an electronics store or from a science supply company)

Instructions
1. Cut an 8-inch by 4-inch strip from the poster board. Fold it in half.
2. Tape two strips of foil to the board, one along each side. The strips of foil should touch when the poster board is folded.

Find a good hiding place for the battery and buzzer. Then make sure the wires will reach the poster board strip from the hiding place. You can use wire cutters or scissors to cut the wire.

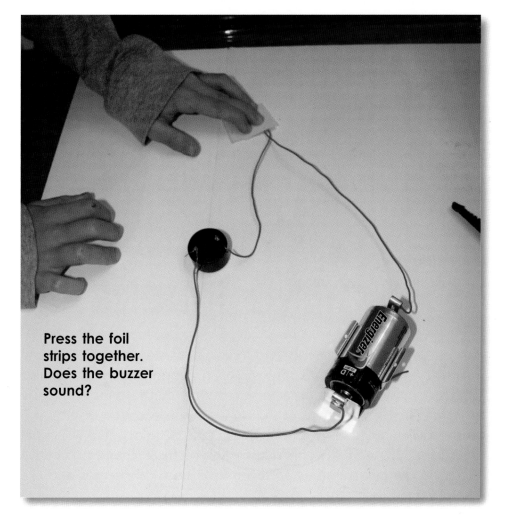

Press the foil strips together. Does the buzzer sound?

3. Tape a piece of wire to the outside of each foil strip.
4. Attach the other end of one wire to one side of the buzzer.
5. Attach the other wire to the positive end of the battery.
6. Connect one more wire from the negative end of the battery to the other end of the buzzer. When you press the poster board together along the fold, the foil pieces will touch. This will complete the circuit and make the buzzer sound.
7. Place the poster board strip under a rug just inside your bedroom door so that one side is on the ground and the other is poised to touch it. When someone walks into your room and steps on the rug, the poster board will come together along the fold. The buzzer will sound and alert you.

EXPLORING MAGNETS

Magnetism is a force that attracts some substances toward others. All magnets have a north and a south pole. Only opposite ends of magnets attract, so north ends are attracted to south ends. Like ends push away from, or repel, each other. For example, a north end of a magnet will push against another magnet's north end. A south end will repel another south end. They act just like electrical charges: negative electrical charges are attracted to positive electrical charges, and like charges repel each other.

The force of a magnet flows like electricity. It moves from the magnet's north pole to its south pole. The area of magnetic flow around the magnet is called its magnetic field.

Some magnets can be very strong, while others are weak. In this activity, you'll have a chance to explore magnets. Find their magnetic fields using iron shavings. Test their strengths with paper clips. Try to make them attract and repel each other.

Materials
- Iron filings (available from science and teacher supply stores; some craft stores may have them as well)
- Magnets of different types (bar, horseshoe, circle) and strengths
- Paper clips

Instructions

1. Use the iron filings to identify the magnetic field for each of your magnets. Draw the different fields for different shaped magnets in a journal or notebook.
2. Place two bar magnets next to each other so that the north pole of one is next to the south pole of the other. Push one closer to the other. What happens?
3. Turn one of the magnets so that the south pole of each is pointed toward the other. What happens when you move one closer to the other?

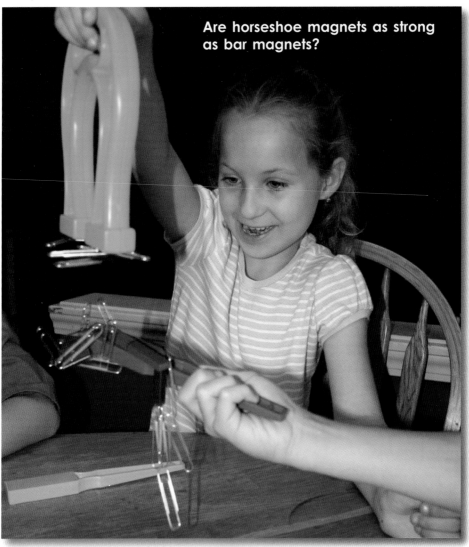

Are horseshoe magnets as strong as bar magnets?

You can buy iron filings in clear plastic containers. They are much easier to use this way.

4. How is this different when you use a horseshoe magnet? A circle magnet?
5. Which of your magnets do you think will be the most powerful? Which do you think will be the least powerful? Put them in order from the strongest to the weakest (in your opinion).
6. Spread the paper clips out on a table. Test the magnets by swirling each one in the pile of paper clips, holding it up, and then counting the paper clips that the magnet picks up. Record you results.
7. Does the size of the magnet make a difference in the number of paper clips it picks up? Why or why not?

Bigger doesn't necessarily mean stronger. Large magnets may be weaker than much smaller ones. However, sometimes size does equal strength. The large magnets that can be found in junkyards are strong enough to pick up cars. They are actually electromagnets, which we'll explore next.

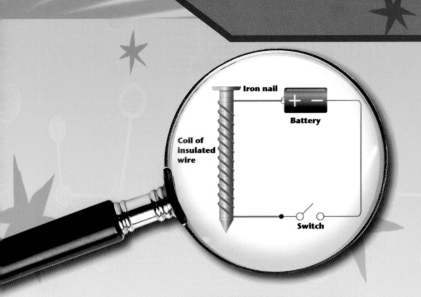

Iron nail

Battery

Coil of insulated wire

Switch

MAKE AN ELECTROMAGNET

In 1820, Hans Christian Oersted accidentally moved an electric wire near a compass. The needle on the compass moved, which means the electrical current had created a magnetic field. A few years later, Michael Faraday discovered that the reverse was true. A magnetic field could generate electricity as well.

Scientists continue to study this relationship. Electricity and magnetism are alike in many ways. They are different as well. A magnetic field always flows into itself. It cannot be separated from its poles. Because of this, you can't use a magnet by itself to power something, like you can a battery. Electricity can flow out and back to itself. This is the characteristic that makes it possible to use electricity to run our toys and household appliances. Another difference between the two is that magnetism can pass through materials that electricity cannot. For example, magnetism can pass through glass and plastic.

An electromagnet is a magnet that is made when an electrical current passes through a wire. When the electricity is turned off, the magnetic field is gone. In this activity, you will create a simple electro-magnet.

Materials
- A long nail or screwdriver
- Insulated wire
- Paper clips
- Battery
- Battery holder

Instructions

1. Wind the wire about 15 to 20 times around the nail or screwdriver.

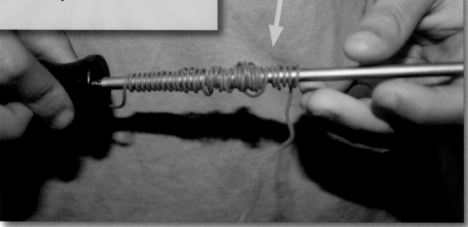

2. Spread the paper clips on a table.
3. Place the battery in the holder.
4. Attach one end of the wire to the positive end of the battery.

5. Attach the other end of the wire to the negative end of the battery.

6. Drag your electromagnet through the paper clip pile.
7. How many paper clips did your electromagnet pick up?
8. Can you figure out a way to increase the magnetism and pick up more paper clips? Try adding another battery or wrapping the wire more or fewer times around the nail.

Test the strength of an electromagnet by counting how many paper clips it can pick up.

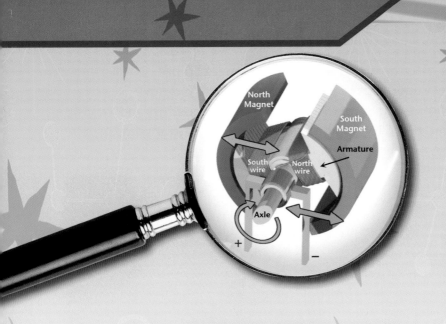

North
Magnet

South
Magnet

Armature

South
wire

North
wire

Axle

+

−

MOTOR ON

Magnets have many uses. They are the main component in compasses. Doors have magnets installed to keep them closed. Astronauts use magnets to secure small objects to the walls of spacecraft. Magnets also allow electric motors to work. When they are placed inside the motor, they create pushing and pulling forces on the armature. The north pole of the magnet pushes the north pole of the armature away, and the south pole pulls it. As the magnets push and pull on the armature, they make it spin, or rotate.

In this activity, you'll use a magnet and a battery to create a simple motor.

Materials	Wire strippers (for adult use)
◆ D-cell battery	◆ **An adult**
◆ Battery holder	◆ Bare wire
◆ Ceramic magnet	◆ Duct tape
◆ Insulated wire	◆ Pencil

Instructions

1. Wind enamel-coated wire around a pencil in 30 tight coils. Leave several inches of extra wire free at each end.

Keep the wire from uncoiling by wrapping the free ends of the wire around the coils.

2. Pull the wire off the pencil, holding it carefully so that it doesn't uncoil.
3. Wrap the free ends of the wire a few times around several coils on either side. Make sure you wrap them opposite of each other.
4. Lay the coil on a table and press it gently so that it is flat, even, and the free ends of the wire lie straight across from each other.
5. Have **an adult** strip the ceramic coating from the free ends of the wire.

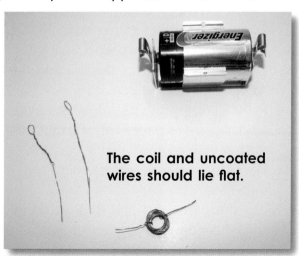

The coil and uncoated wires should lie flat.

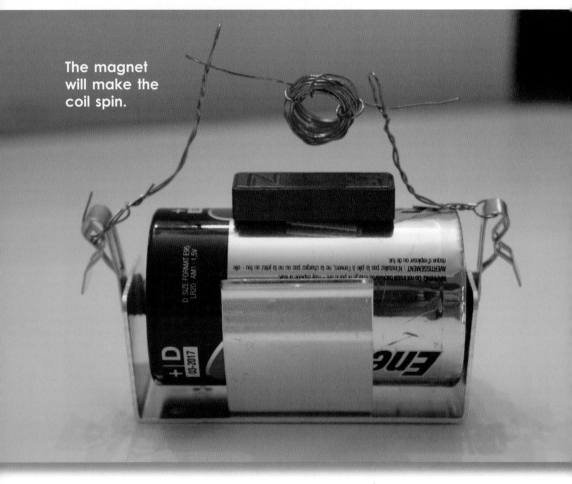

The magnet will make the coil spin.

6. Use two pieces of bare wire to make handles for the coil.
7. Bend each piece around the pencil to make a loop.
8. Attach the handles to the holes in the battery holder. If you want, secure them with duct tape.
9. Insert the free ends of the coil into the loops you created on each handle.
10. Put the battery into its holder, blocking one of the connections with a small piece of paper. This will block the current until you are ready to start your motor.
11. Place the ceramic magnet on top of the battery holder just underneath the coil.
12. Pull the paper out and give your coil a spin to get it started. It should continue to spin faster and faster.

BUILD A MAGLEV TRAIN

Magnetism makes some interesting things possible. Artwork and reminders can be hung on refrigerators. Motors can be powered. And, amazingly, when like poles repel each other, things can float in midair. They ride on the magnetic field. This is called magnetic levitation, or maglev.

Maglev technology is being used in countries like Japan to power super-high-speed trains. These trains can reach speeds of over 300 miles per hour (482 kilometers per hour)—one set a record in 2003 of 361 miles per hour (581 kilometers per hour). A maglev train hovers above a single track. It moves using the attraction and repelling forces of magnets. It can travel so fast because there is no friction to slow it down.

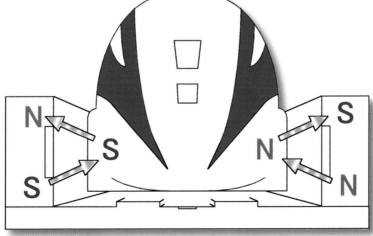

Use your own magnets to see if you can build a small maglev train of your own. You may need to experiment with the placement of your magnets. The balance of magnetic forces needs to be perfect to hold the train steady in midair.

Materials
- 24 small magnets
- Double-sided tape
- Poster board
- Small foam board
- Sheet of plastic cut in half lengthwise
- Modeling clay

Instructions

1. Place two strips of tape on the poster board in parallel lines about an inch apart.
2. Arrange 10 magnets on each strip of tape, equally spread out. Make sure the same pole of all magnets are pointed up. This will be your "track."
3. To keep the train on its track, use the plastic pieces to create walls. Stick the plastic to the poster board with modeling clay to hold it upright. Your track will resemble an open-topped box.

The magnets on the track will repel the magnets on the train, keeping the train in motion.

4. Cut a small rectangle of foam board so that it fits exactly inside the guide walls.
5. Attach a magnet to each corner of the rectangle. If your track has all north poles facing up, be sure the magnets on the train have the north poles facing down so that the train will be repelled.
6. Place your train gently above the track and let it go. It should float.
7. Give your train a gentle push and watch it continue to move toward the other end.

Books

Adamczyk, Peter, Paul-Francis Law, Jane Chisholm, and Eliot Humberstone. *Electricity and Magnetism*. Tulsa, OK: EDC, 2007.

Bailey, Jacqui, and Matthew Lilly. *Charged Up: The Story of Electricity*. Minneapolis: Picture Window, 2006.

Claybourne, Anna, and Kevin Hopgood. *The Shocking Story of Electricity*. London: Usborne, 2006.

Gardner, Robert. *Easy Genius Science Projects with Electricity and Magnetism*. New Jersey: Enslow Publishers, Inc., 2009.

O'Donnell, Liam. *Shocking World of Electricity with Max Axiom, Super Scientist*. Minneapolis: Capstone Press, 2007.

Padilla, Michael J. *Prentice Hall Science Explorer: Electricity and Magnetism*. New Jersey: Pearson Prentice Hall, 2006.

Parker, Steve. *Electricity*. London: DK, 2005.

Works Consulted

Bodanis, David. *Electric Universe: The Shocking True Story of Electricity*. New York: Crown, 2005.

Hiroko Tabuchi. "Japan Envisions a New Destination for Its Trains: The U.S." *International Herald Tribune,* November 3, 2010.

Jonnes, Jill. *Empires of Light: Edison, Tesla, Westinghouse, and the Race to Electrify the World*. New York: Random House, 2004.

Toor, Amar. "China's Bullet Train Sets World Record for High-Speed Train Travel." *Switched.com,* September 30, 2010. http://www.switched. com/2010/09/30/chinas-bullet-train-sets-world-record-for-high- speed-train-trav?icid=sphere_blogsmith_inpage_engadget

Van Valkenburgh, Nooger and Neville. *Basic Electricity*. Clifton Park, NY: Delmar Cengage Learning, 2007.

Verschuur, Gerrit L. *Hidden Attraction: The Mystery and History of Magnetism*. Oxford: Oxford University Press, 1996.

Wolfe, Joe. "Electric Motors and Generators." The University of New South Wales. http://www.animations.physics.unsw.edu.au//jw/ electricmotors.html

On the Internet

California Energy Commission, Energy Quest: "The Energy Story"
    http://energyquest.ca.gov/story/index.html

EIA Energy Kids: Electricity
    http://www.eia.doe.gov/kids/energy.cfm?page=
    electricity_home-basics

The Electric Ben Franklin: "Ben Franklin and His Electric Kite"
    http://www.ushistory.org/franklin/info/kite.htm

Kids Konnect: Magnets
    http://www.kidskonnect.com/subject-index/15-science/
    90-magnets.html

Science Supply Companies

Home Science Tools: Physical Science and Physics
    http://www.hometrainingtools.com/physical-science-physics/c/4/

Science Kit Store
    http://sciencekitstore.com/

Science Kit & Boreal Laboratories
    http://sciencekit.com/

Steve Spangler Science Store: "Electricity and Energy"
    http://www.stevespanglerscience.com/category/electricity-energy

Steve Spangler Science Store: "Magnetism"
    http://www.stevespanglerscience.com/category/magnetism

PHOTO CREDITS: Cover, p. 1 —Joe Rasemas; pp. 4, 5, 6, 7, 8, 10, 16, 18, 21, 24, 26, 29, 32, 35, 38, 41—cc-by-sa; pp. 11, 12, 13, 14, 15, 17, 19, 20, 22, 23, 25, 27, 28, 30, 31, 33, 34, 36, 37, 39, 40, 42, 43—Colleen Kessler. Every effort has been made to locate all copyright holders of material used in this book. If any errors or omissions have occurred, corrections will be made in future editions of the book.

atom (AA-tum)—The smallest part of an element that still holds its properties. Each contains at least one proton and one electron.

charge—An amount of electrical energy, especially the gain or loss of electrons in a body.

circuit (SIR-kit)—The path through which electricity flows, which usually includes the source of electrical energy.

conductor (kun-DUK-tur)—A substance that allows energy to transfer, including electricity to flow.

current (KUR-unt)—The flow of electric charge; the rate of electric flow.

electricity (ee-lek-TRIH-sih-tee)—A form of energy transferred by the movement of electrons.

electron (ee-LEK-tron)—A small particle with a negative charge that balances protons in atoms.

electroscope (ee-LEK-troh-skohp)—An instrument used to detect electrical charge.

filament (FIH-luh-munt)—A long, thin piece of material, such as carbon or platinum, that glows when electricity passes through it.

friction (FRIK-shun)—A force between two surfaces that acts in the opposite direction of motion.

incandescent (in-kan-DEH-sent)—Giving off enough heat to produce visible light.

induction (in-DUK-shun)—The act of causing electricity to flow.

insulator (IN-suh-lay-tor)—Something that prevents energy transfer, including the flow of electricity.

magnetic levitation (mag-NEH-tik leh-vih-TAY-shun)—*Maglev* for short, a system that uses magnets to lift and propel, as in maglev trains.

magnetism (MAG-nuh-tism)—The force that attracts or repels some objects toward or away from other objects.

motor (MOH-tur)—A machine that converts electrical energy into motion.

neutron (NOO-tron)—A small particle with a neutral charge (neither positive or negative).

proton (PROH-ton)—A small particle with a positive charge that balances electrons in atoms.

repel (ree-PEL)—To push away without touching.

static electricity (STAA-tik ee-lek-TRIH-sih-tee)—Electricity made of motionless charges, which are produced by friction.

Colleen Kessler is the author of several science books for kids, including *A Project Guide to Reptiles and Birds, A Project Guide to the Solar System, A Project Guide to Forces and Motion,* and *A Project Guide to Light and Optics* for Mitchell Lane Publishers. A former teacher of gifted students, Colleen now satisfies her curiosity as a full-time nonfiction writer. She does her researching and writing in her home office overlooking a wooded backyard in Northeastern Ohio. You can often find her blasting off rockets or searching for salamanders with her husband, Brian, and kids, Trevor, Molly, and Logan, or talking to schoolchildren about the excitement of studying science and nature. For more information about her books and presentations, or to invite her for a school visit, check out her web site at http://www.colleen-kessler.com.